Little People, BIG DREAMS™

FLORENCE NIGHTINGALE

Written by
Maria Isabel Sánchez Vegara

Illustrated by
Kelsey Garrity-Riley

Frances Lincoln
Children's Books

Long ago, there was a wealthy British girl named after the Italian city where she was born—Florence. Her parents soon realized that their little daughter had not just a brilliant mind, but the kindest heart in the world.

Her father was a man ahead of his time, and gave his daughters the finest education. He took them on long tours around Europe. Every time they arrived at a new city, Florence was fascinated to see the hospitals there.

Florence grew to become an extraordinary young lady who felt happier visiting the sick and the poor in her village than attending a fancy dance to look for a husband. She soon realized that taking care of others was her calling.

When Florence told her family that she wanted to be a nurse, everyone disagreed. At that time, not even poor widows would want to work in a hospital! All that was expected from her was to get married and live a comfortable life for ever after.

But that wasn't Florence's plan! She kept studying in secret. When she was old enough, she went to Germany, where she learned all about nursing from Pastor Theodor and his committed team. She kept a note of every single discovery!

Back in London, Florence took a job as a head nurse at a hospital for women. In a few weeks, she showed that being in charge was not just about giving your best, but about helping everyone else to do the same.

A horrible war broke out in the Black Sea, and thousands of young soldiers were sent to fight far away from home. It wasn't long until terrible news arrived. The army hospitals were full of injured men who needed urgent help!

Without hesitation, Florence organized a group of 38 volunteer nurses. It included 15 brave nuns, and her aunt Mai. With just a few days' notice, they sailed away to Constantinople, ready to assist the soldiers with patience, diligence, and kindness.

Nothing had prepared Florence and her nurses for what they found. That hospital was the darkest and dirtiest place they had ever been to! It was in such terrible condition that, instead of getting better, injured soldiers were getting ill.

Florence started by telling all doctors to wash their hands before assisting a patient. She asked the healthiest people to scrub the hospital from floor to ceiling. Her recipe of fresh air, sunlight, healthy food, and clean linens did the rest!

Thousands of men were saved thanks to Florence.
They called her The Lady of the Lamp, and back home,
everyone was waiting to meet her—even Queen Victoria!

She rewarded Florence with a precious brooch
and a big amount of money.

Florence used every single penny to open a hospital and a training school for future nurses. She also wrote a book for those who wanted to learn the secrets of her profession, turning nursing into a job that was respected.

And every May, for little Florence's birthday, the whole world celebrates International Nurses Day.

HAPPY INTERNATIO

A date to honor the mother of modern nursing, and the work of all the brave nurses shining a light on us all.

NAL NURSES DAY

FLORENCE NIGHTINGALE

(Born 1820 – Died 1910)

1838   1845

Florence Nightingale was born on 12th May 1820, in Florence, Italy. The family returned to Britain a year later, and the little girl spent her childhood in Hampshire and Derbyshire. Her father gave his two daughters a good education, and Florence excelled at science and languages. She knew from an early age that rather than living the life of comfort that was expected for her, she wanted to care for others. After turning down a marriage proposal, she traveled the world and trained to be a nurse in Germany, much to the dismay of her family. Upon returning to London in 1853, she took an unpaid position as the superintendent at a hospital for women. When the Crimean War began in March 1854, Florence oversaw the introduction of nurses to military hospitals. She arrived in Constantinople, today known

c. 1880s   1898

as Istanbul, along with 38 nurses. The hospitals there were so unhygienic, soldiers who might have survived their wounds were dying from diseases, such as cholera and typhoid, created by the unsanitary conditions. Florence made sure that the hospitals were sanitised and ventilated, and that soliders had good food and clean water. These changes saved thousands of lives and began a medical revolution. Back home in Britain, Florence was nicknamed "The Lady of the Lamp" by *The Times* newspaper, and her methods were adopted in hospitals across the country. Later in life, she opened a training school for nurses and wrote a book, *Notes on Nursing*. Florence, the mother of modern healthcare, taught the world to honor and respect the hard work of our nurses.

Want to find out more about **Florence Nightingale?**

Have a read of these great books:

DK Life Stories: Florence Nightingale by Kitson Jazynka

Vlad and the Florence Nightingale Adventure by Kate Cunningham

Brimming with creative inspiration, how-to projects, and useful information to enrich your everyday life, quarto.com is a favorite destination for those pursuing their interests and passions.

Text © 2022 Maria Isabel Sánchez Vegara. Illustrations © 2022 Kelsey Garrity-Riley.

Original concept of the series by Maria Isabel Sánchez Vegara, published by Alba Editorial, SLU.

Little People Big Dreams and Pequeña&Grande are registered trademarks of Alba Editorial, SLU for books, publications and e-books. Produced under licence from Alba Editorial, SLU

First Published in the USA in 2021 by Frances Lincoln Children's Books, an imprint of The Quarto Group.

Quarto Boston North Shore, 100 Cummings Center, Suite 265D, Beverly, MA 01915, USA

Tel: +1 978-282-9590, Fax: +1 978-283-2742 **www.Quarto.com**

A catalogue record for this book is available from the British Library.

ISBN 978-0-7112-7079-4

Set in Futura BT.

Published by Katie Cotton • Designed by Sasha Moxon

Edited by Lucy Menzies • Production by Nikki Ingram

Editorial Assistance from Rachel Robinson

Manufactured in Guangdong, China CC122021

1 3 5 7 9 8 6 4 2

Photographic acknowledgements (pages 28-29, from left to right): 1. Florence Nightingale, 1820-1910. Pioneer of nursing and a reformer of hospital sanitation methods. Engraved by Mote after G. Staal. From the book "World Noted Women" by Mary Cowden Clarke, published 1858. © Universal Images Group via Getty Images. 2. English nursing reformer Florence Nightingale (1820 - 1910), who became the first woman to receive the Order of Merit for her tireless efforts during the Crimean War. © Hulton Archive via Getty Images. 3. Florence Nightingale (1820-1910), photograph ca. 1880 © Everett Collection via Shutterstock Images 4. Florence Nightingale original glass negative c1898 © David Riley via Alamy Stock Photo

Collect the Little People, BIG DREAMS™ series:

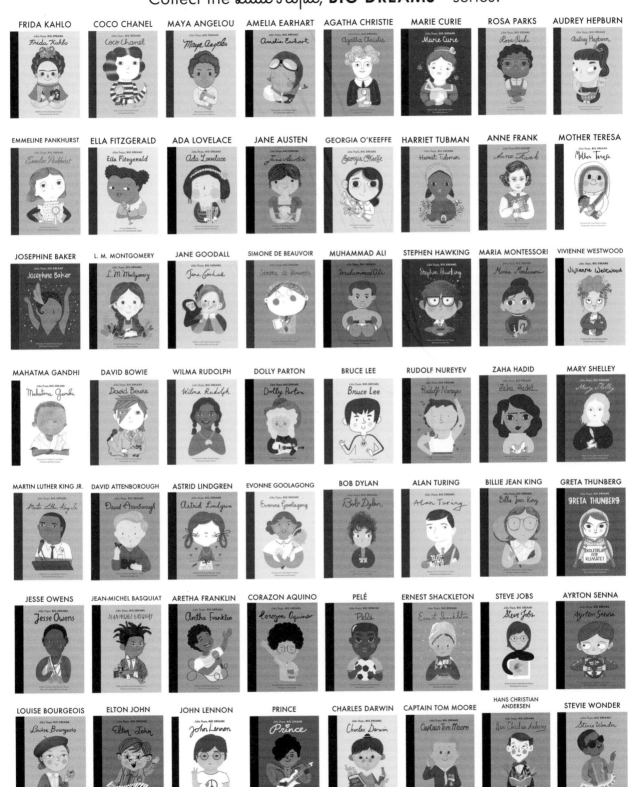

FRIDA KAHLO	COCO CHANEL	MAYA ANGELOU	AMELIA EARHART	AGATHA CHRISTIE	MARIE CURIE	ROSA PARKS	AUDREY HEPBURN
EMMELINE PANKHURST	ELLA FITZGERALD	ADA LOVELACE	JANE AUSTEN	GEORGIA O'KEEFFE	HARRIET TUBMAN	ANNE FRANK	MOTHER TERESA
JOSEPHINE BAKER	L. M. MONTGOMERY	JANE GOODALL	SIMONE DE BEAUVOIR	MUHAMMAD ALI	STEPHEN HAWKING	MARIA MONTESSORI	VIVIENNE WESTWOOD
MAHATMA GANDHI	DAVID BOWIE	WILMA RUDOLPH	DOLLY PARTON	BRUCE LEE	RUDOLF NUREYEV	ZAHA HADID	MARY SHELLEY
MARTIN LUTHER KING JR.	DAVID ATTENBOROUGH	ASTRID LINDGREN	EVONNE GOOLAGONG	BOB DYLAN	ALAN TURING	BILLIE JEAN KING	GRETA THUNBERG
JESSE OWENS	JEAN-MICHEL BASQUIAT	ARETHA FRANKLIN	CORAZON AQUINO	PELÉ	ERNEST SHACKLETON	STEVE JOBS	AYRTON SENNA
LOUISE BOURGEOIS	ELTON JOHN	JOHN LENNON	PRINCE	CHARLES DARWIN	CAPTAIN TOM MOORE	HANS CHRISTIAN ANDERSEN	STEVIE WONDER

MEGAN RAPINOE	MARY ANNING	MALALA YOUSAFZAI	ANDY WARHOL	RUPAUL	MICHELLE OBAMA	MINDY KALING	IRIS APFEL
ROSALIND FRANKLIN	RUTH BADER GINSBURG	MARILYN MONROE	KAMALA HARRIS	ALBERT EINSTEIN	CHARLES DICKENS	YOKO ONO	MICHAEL JORDAN
NELSON MANDELA	PABLO PICASSO	AMANDA GORMAN	GLORIA STEINEM	FLORENCE NIGHTINGALE	HARRY HOUDINI	J.R.R. TOLKIEN	

ACTIVITY BOOKS

STICKER ACTIVITY BOOK

COLORING BOOK

LITTLE ME, BIG DREAMS JOURNAL

Discover more about the series at www.littlepeoplebigdreams.com